FIRST 50 SONGS
YOU SHOULD PLAY ON THE BASSOON

ISBN 978-1-5400-7006-7

HAL•LEONARD®

Visit Hal Leonard Online at
www.halleonard.com

Contact us:
Hal Leonard
7777 West Bluemound Road
Milwaukee, WI 53213
Email: info@halleonard.com

In Europe, contact:
Hal Leonard Europe Limited
42 Wigmore Street
Marylebone, London, W1U 2RN
Email: info@halleonardeurope.com

In Australia, contact:
Hal Leonard Australia Pty. Ltd.
4 Lentara Court
Cheltenham, Victoria, 3192 Australia
Email: info@halleonard.com.au

ALL OF ME

BASSOON

Words and Music by JOHN STEPHENS
and TOBY GAD

Slowly, in 2

3

ALL YOU NEED IS LOVE

BASSOON

Words and Music by JOHN LENNON
and PAUL McCARTNEY

AMAZING GRACE

BASSOON

Traditional American Melody

BASIN STREET BLUES

BASSOON

Words and Music by
SPENCER WILLIAMS

(small notes optional)

BEST SONG EVER

BASSOON

Words and Music by EDWARD DREWETT,
WAYNE HECTOR, JULIAN BUNETTA
and JOHN RYAN

BEER BARREL POLKA
(Roll Out the Barrel)
Based on the European success "Skoda Lasky"*

BASSOON

By LEW BROWN, WLADIMIR A. TIMM,
JAROMIR VEJVODA and VASEK ZEMAN

CARNIVAL OF VENICE

BASSOON

By JULIUS BENEDICT

Moderately, with motion

CIRCLE OF LIFE

from THE LION KING

BASSOON

Music by ELTON JOHN
Lyrics by TIM RICE

DOWN ON THE CORNER

BASSOON

Words and Music by
JOHN FOGERTY

Brightly, in 2

THE ELEPHANT
from CARNIVAL OF THE ANIMALS

BASSOON

By CAMILLE SAINT-SAËNS

EVERMORE

from BEAUTY AND THE BEAST

BASSOON

Music by ALAN MENKEN
Lyrics by TIM RICE

FLY ME TO THE MOON
(In Other Words)

BASSOON

Words and Music by
BART HOWARD

FIGHT SONG

BASSOON

Words and Music by RACHEL PLATTEN
and DAVE BASSETT

CODA

D.S. al Coda

THE FOOL ON THE HILL

Words and Music by JOHN LENNON
and PAUL McCARTNEY

BASSOON

Slowly

GOD BLESS AMERICA®

BASSOON

Words and Music by
IRVING BERLIN

THE GODFATHER
(Love Theme)
from the Paramount Picture THE GODFATHER

BASSOON

By NINO ROTA

Slowly and expressively

HALLELUJAH

BASSOON

Words and Music by
LEONARD COHEN

Moderately slow, in 2

HAPPY
from DESPICABLE ME 2

BASSOON

Words and Music by
PHARRELL WILLIAMS

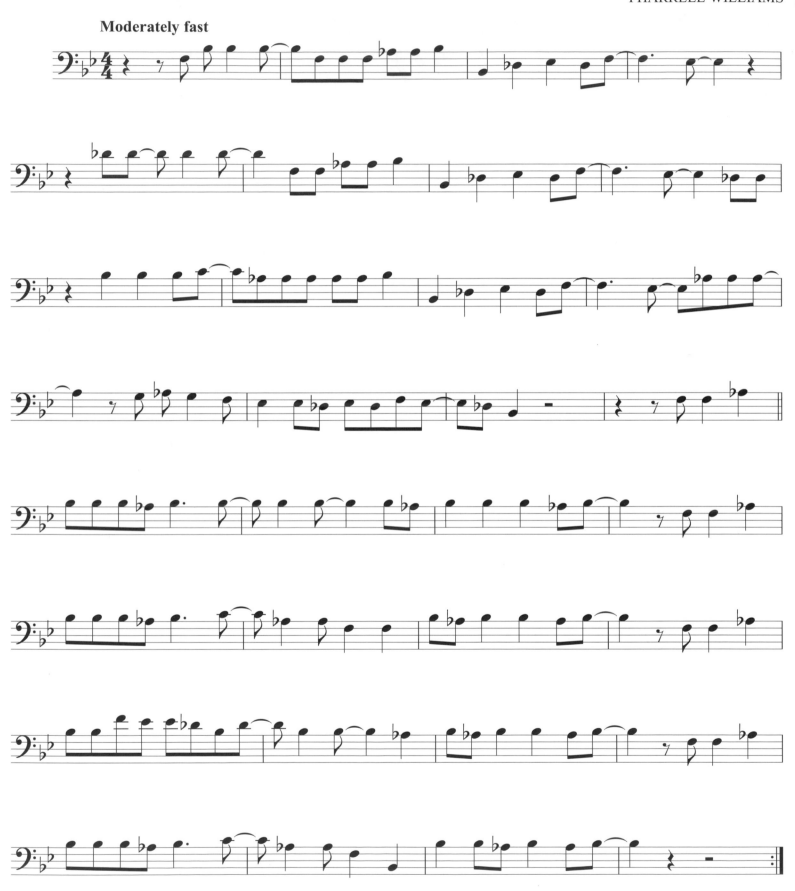

HELLO

BASSOON

Words and Music by
LIONEL RICHIE

Slow Ballad

HELLO, DOLLY!

from HELLO, DOLLY!

BASSOON

Music and Lyric by
JERRY HERMAN

HEY JUDE

BASSOON

Words and Music by JOHN LENNON
and PAUL McCARTNEY

HOW DEEP IS YOUR LOVE

from the Motion Picture SATURDAY NIGHT FEVER

Bassoon

Words and Music by BARRY GIBB,
ROBIN GIBB and MAURICE GIBB

I WILL ALWAYS LOVE YOU

BASSOON

Words and Music by
DOLLY PARTON

Moderately slow

small notes optional

IN THE HALL OF THE MOUNTAIN KING

from PEER GYNT

BASSOON

By EDVARD GRIEG

THEME FROM "JAWS"

from the Universal Picture JAWS

BASSOON

By JOHN WILLIAMS

Moderately

Repeat and Fade

JUST GIVE ME A REASON

BASSOON

Words and Music by ALECIA MOORE,
JEFF BHASKER and NATE RUESS

JUST THE WAY YOU ARE

BASSOON

Words and Music by BRUNO MARS,
ARI LEVINE, PHILIP LAWRENCE,
KHARI CAIN and KHALIL WALTON

Moderately

LET IT GO
from FROZEN

BASSOON

Music and Lyrics by KRISTEN ANDERSON-LOPEZ
and ROBERT LOPEZ

LIVIN' ON A PRAYER

BASSOON

Words and Music by JON BON JOVI,
DESMOND CHILD and RICHIE SAMBORA

Moderate Rock

Repeat and Fade

MAS QUE NADA

BASSOON

Words and Music by
JORGE BEN

MY HEART WILL GO ON

(Love Theme from 'Titanic')

from the Paramount and Twentieth Century Fox Motion Picture TITANIC

BASSOON

Music by JAMES HORNER
Lyric by WILL JENNINGS

Moderately

THE PINK PANTHER

from THE PINK PANTHER

Bassoon

By HENRY MANCINI

Moderately, mysterioso

NIGHT TRAIN

BASSOON

Words by OSCAR WASHINGTON
and LEWIS C. SIMPKINS
Music by JIMMY FORREST

PETER GUNN
Theme Song from the Television Series

BASSOON

By HENRY MANCINI

PURE IMAGINATION
from WILLY WONKA AND THE CHOCOLATE FACTORY

BASSOON

Words and Music by LESLIE BRICUSSE
and ANTHONY NEWLEY

ROAR

BASSOON

Words and Music by KATY PERRY, MAX MARTIN, DR. LUKE, BONNIE McKEE and HENRY WALTER

Moderately

ROLLING IN THE DEEP

BASSOON

Words and Music by ADELE ADKINS
and PAUL EPWORTH

SATIN DOLL

BASSOON

By DUKE ELLINGTON

SEE YOU AGAIN

from FURIOUS 7

Bassoon

Words and Music by CAMERON THOMAZ,
CHARLIE PUTH, JUSTIN FRANKS,
ANDREW CEDAR, DANN HUME,
JOSH HARDY and PHOEBE COCKBURN

SHAKE IT OFF

BASSOON

Words and Music by TAYLOR SWIFT,
MAX MARTIN and SHELLBACK

THE SORCERER'S APPRENTICE
(Theme)
from FANTASIA

BASSOON

By PAUL DUKAS

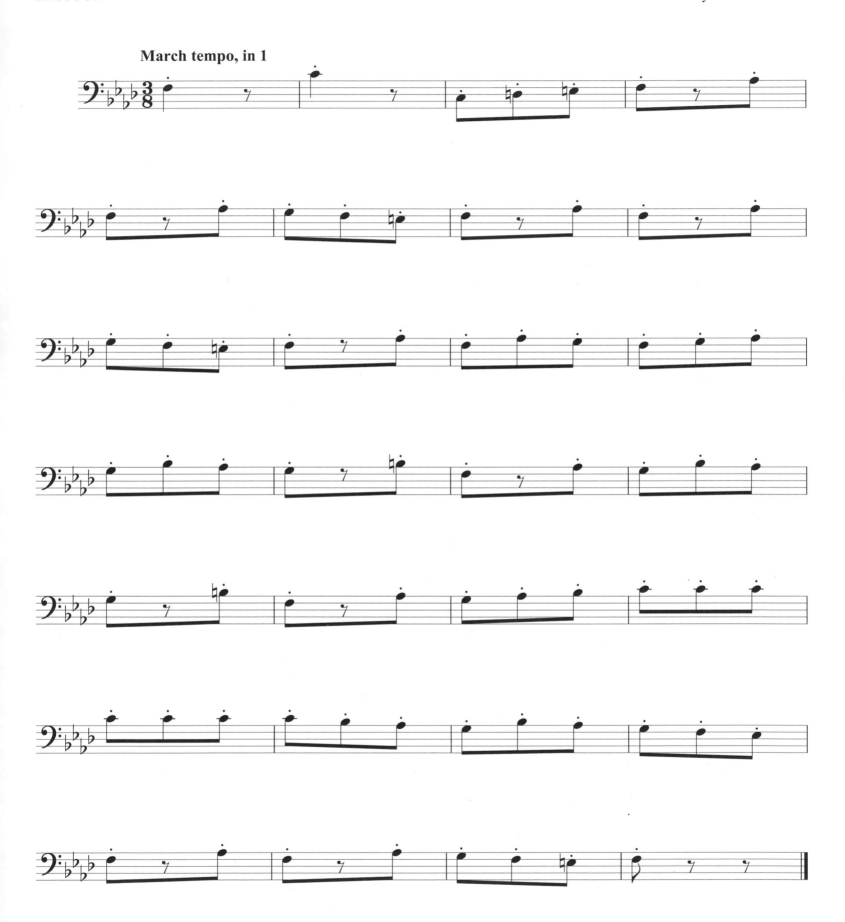

STAND BY ME

BASSOON

Words and Music by JERRY LEIBER,
MIKE STOLLER and BEN E. KING

THE STAR-SPANGLED BANNER

BASSOON

Words by FRANCIS SCOTT KEY
Music by JOHN STAFFORD SMITH

STAY WITH ME

BASSOON

Words and Music by SAM SMITH,
JAMES NAPIER, WILLIAM EDWARD PHILLIPS,
TOM PETTY and JEFF LYNNE

STOMPIN' AT THE SAVOY

BASSOON

By BENNY GOODMAN,
EDGAR SAMPSON and CHICK WEBB

Bright Swing

STRANGERS IN THE NIGHT

BASSOON

Words by CHARLES SINGLETON and EDDIE SNYDER
Music by BERT KAEMPFERT

Moderately slow

SUMMERTIME
from PORGY AND BESS®

Bassoon

Music and Lyrics by GEORGE GERSHWIN,
DuBOSE and DOROTHY HEYWARD
and IRA GERSHWIN

THIS IS ME
from THE GREATEST SHOWMAN

BASSOON

Words and Music by BENJ PASEK
and JUSTIN PAUL

Defiantly

UPTOWN FUNK

Bassoon

Words and Music by MARK RONSON,
BRUNO MARS, PHILIP LAWRENCE, JEFF BHASKER, DEVON GALLASPY,
NICHOLAUS WILLIAMS, LONNIE SIMMONS, RONNIE WILSON,
CHARLES WILSON, RUDOLPH TAYLOR and ROBERT WILSON

WHAT A WONDERFUL WORLD

BASSOON

Words and Music by GEORGE DAVID WEISS
and BOB THIELE